BUTTERFLIES AND MOTHS
around the World

Eveline Jourdan

BUTTERFLIES AND MOTHS
around the World

Lerner Publications Company
Minneapolis, Minnesota

The publisher wishes to thank Ronald L. Huber, Entomologist, The Science Museum of Minnesota, and Jerry W. Heaps, Department of Entomology, The University of Minnesota, for their assistance in the preparation of this book.

Cover photograph © by Tom Stack and Associates

LIBRARY OF CONGRESS CATALOGING IN PUBLICATION DATA

Jourdan, Eveline.
   Butterflies and moths around the world.

   (A Nature and man book)
   Translation of Bunte Schmetterlingswelt.
   SUMMARY: Outlines the life cycle of moths and butterflies and discusses the specific habits and characteristics of more than 50 of these abundant insects.

   1. Butterflies—Juvenile literature. 2. Moths—Juvenile literature. [1. Butterflies. 2. Moths] I. Title.

QL544.2.J68   1981   595.78′9   80-20086
ISBN 0-8225-0567-3

This edition first published 1981 by Lerner Publications Company, Minneapolis, Minnesota.
English translation by Carolyn Olstead. All English language rights reserved.
Original edition copyright © MCMLXXV by Deutsche Verlags-Anstalt, Stuttgart, West Germany.

International Standard Book Number: 0-8225-0567-3
Library of Congress Catalog Card Number: 80-20086

Manufactured in the United States of America

CONTENTS

Giant sulphur butterflies (genus *Phoebis*)

PREFACE

Butterflies and moths make up a large part of the more than 800,000 known types of insects existing on earth. Researchers have described and named nearly 100,000 different species (kinds) of Lepidoptera, the scientific order to which butterflies and moths belong. In fact, some scientists have estimated that of all the kinds of animals in the world, one out of every ten is a species of butterfly or moth.

Butterflies and moths have fascinated people for centuries, and there have been many legends and stories about them. In the fourth century B.C., the Greek philosopher and scientist Aristotle studied the development of the butterfly. He may have been the first person to use the Greek word *psyche* to mean both "butterfly" and "human soul." It seems to have been a common belief in Aristotle's time that while people slept, their souls left their bodies through their mouths,

taking the form of butterflies and roaming about.

The butterfly was also a symbol of immortality for the people of ancient times. It was believed to represent the souls of the dead, perhaps because flocks of butterflies often gathered around the flowers used to decorate graves. To the Aztec Indians of ancient America, the butterfly was also a symbol of a soul that had escaped from the mouth of a dead person. Often butterflies were seen as representing the souls of Aztec warriors who had died on the battlefield.

The people of ancient times were not the only ones who had superstitious beliefs about butterflies. The idea of butterflies representing souls continued through the entire Middle Ages and survives even today. In some regions of Ireland, people still believe that a white butterfly or moth is the soul of a sinless person on its way to paradise. If,

Mourning cloak butterfly *(Nymphalis antiopa)*

however, the wings of the insect are spotted, the soul is condemned to pay for its sins in purgatory. In some parts of Africa, the butterfly is believed to represent not just the soul after death, but the whole cycle of human life. In childhood, a person is like a small caterpillar, and in adulthood, a large caterpillar. In old age, a human being changes into a pupa enclosed in a hard shell. The shell is the grave, from which the soul finally escapes in the form of an adult butterfly.

Even the origin of the word *butterfly* seems to be connected with legend and superstition. In the Middle Ages, many people in Europe believed in witches, who were sometimes thought to take the form of butterflies. Disguised in this way, they were supposed to fly into people's houses to steal butter and milk. This legend may be the origin of the butterfly's name. Another theory is that the insect was given its name because so many species of butterflies are bright yellow in color. Both of these explanations are possible, but in fact no one really knows where the butterfly got its unusual name.

Individual species of butterflies and moths also have strange and sometimes beautiful names. In North America, there are butterflies called painted lady, mourning cloak, dogface, and swallowtail. The moth group includes tiger moths and puss moths, lobster moths and hawk moths. Such names are charming, but they can also be confusing because the same insect often has a different common name in different parts of the world. For example, the butterfly known as the mourning cloak in North America is called the Camberwell beauty in England. Luckily, each species of butterfly and moth has a scientific name—usually in Latin—by which it is known throughout the world. When scientists talk about the mourning cloak/ Camberwell beauty, they call it *Nymphalis antiopa* so that there can be no mistake about the butterfly's identity. They may also refer to the insect's family name—Nymphalidae—to indicate its relationship to other butterflies. In this book, you will find butterflies and moths identified by their scientific names as well as their most familiar common names.

The Life Cycle of Butterflies and Moths

Human beings have always been fascinated not only by the beauty of butterflies and moths, but also by their unique process of development. Today, after centuries of study and observation, we know a great deal about the life cycles of these insects. The remarkable process has been given the name *metamorphosis* (met-uh-MOR-fuh-sis), a combination of Greek words meaning "transformation."

Like all insects, butterflies and moths begin their lives as *eggs*. The eggs of different species vary in shape; some are round or oval, while others are shaped like cones, cucumbers, or pears. Butterfly and moth eggs are usually pale yellow or green in color, but a few species have bright red or green eggs. Most eggs are quite small in size, the largest probably not more than .10 of an inch (2.5 millimeters) in diameter.

The number of eggs produced at one time is another factor that varies from species to species. Most female butterflies lay an average of 100 to 200 eggs, but female moths of the root borer family produce 30,000 eggs. The lambda moth (family Noctuidae) can lay 1,000 eggs within a few days, whereas the large puss moth *(Cerura vinula)* lays only 2 eggs at a time.

There is also a great variety in their methods of laying eggs. Some butterflies and moths deposit their eggs on the particular kind of plant that will provide their offspring with food. The females somehow locate the right plants, perhaps by smell, and lay their eggs on the leaves or stems, gluing them on with a sticky fluid produced by their bodies. Other butterflies and moths insert their eggs into crevices in trees or plants, where they will be safe from danger. The gold-tail moth of the family Lymantriidae provides

A greatly enlarged photograph showing eggs on a leaf

special protection for her eggs by covering them with a layer of hairs brushed off the tip of her abdomen. Some species, however, are much less careful; they lay their eggs while in flight, letting them fall where they may.

The length of time that the eggs take to hatch can range anywhere from a few days to several months, depending on the species and on other factors such as weather conditions. When the eggs finally do hatch, the creatures that emerge are *caterpillars,* the second or larval stage in the life cycle of butterflies and moths.

Most caterpillars, or larvae (LAR-vee), are more or less worm-like in form, but when they are fully developed, they have an amazing variety of skin coverings and colors. There are some caterpillars with smooth, bare skin and others covered with bushy hair. Many caterpillars have bumps, bristles, horns, and knobs on various parts of their bodies. Their colors range from pale browns and grays to brilliant greens, yellows, and reds in patterns of stripes and blotches. All of these features help to protect caterpillars from

enemies by making them hard to see or so frightening in appearance that predators leave them alone.

Despite the differences in their appearances, all caterpillars have the same basic structure. Their bodies are made up of 13 ring-like sections, or *segments.* The 1st segment contains the head, which is equipped with a strong set of jaws designed for biting and chewing food. On each of the next 3 segments is a pair of short, jointed legs, each with a sharp claw at its tip. Most caterpillars have pairs of so-called false legs on the 7th through the 10th segments of their bodies. These "legs" are not jointed and have groups of tiny hooks at their tips. On the last segment of the caterpillar's body is another pair of leg-like structures usually called *claspers.* This variety of "legs" enables the caterpillar to cling to the leaves and stems of plants and to move from place to place.

When caterpillars are on the move, they are seeking only one thing: food. They spend all their time eating and storing enough nourishment so that the next stage of meta-morphosis can take place. Immediately after

The caterpillar of a puss moth

hatching, caterpillars begin by devouring their own eggshells. Then they seek out more solid food.

Some caterpillars are very particular and will eat only one kind of green plant; others feed on a wide variety of trees and plants. When large numbers of hungry caterpillars attack living plants, they can do a great deal of damage. Certain kinds of caterpillars feed on nonliving things, such as the bodies of dead animals or materials of animal origin, for instance, hide, feathers, fur, and wool. In this group are the caterpillars of the clothes moth *(Tineola bisselliella)*, which often find their food in the closets of people's houses. There are even some caterpillars that will eat each other when nothing better is at hand.

With all the eating that they do, caterpillars grow very rapidly. That is, their bodies grow, but their skins do not. In order to continue developing, caterpillars must get rid of their old skins several times during their existence. This process is called *molting.* The old skin splits and comes off, revealing a new, roomier skin underneath. Most caterpillars molt 4 or 5 times, although some species of moths shed their skins at least 12 times.

When a caterpillar molts for the last time, it becomes a *pupa* (PEW-pah), the third stage in the life cycle of butterflies and moths. Different species prepare for this important step in different ways. Most butterfly caterpillars find themselves a place on a leaf or branch and begin to send out a stream of sticky liquid from an opening near their mouths. This liquid sticks to the plant and quickly hardens to form a kind of silk pad or button. The caterpillar hangs head downward from this pad, firmly attached to the plant, while it sheds its skin for the last time. When the skin splits and falls away, the pupa inside is revealed. The pupa is soft at first, but a hard shell, called a *chrysalis,* immediately begins to form over it. Within the protection of the chrysalis, the body of the pupa will change into that of an adult butterfly.

Many moth *pupae* (the plural of *pupa,* pronounced PEW-pee) are protected by a silken case called a *cocoon,* which they spin

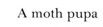
A moth pupa

around their bodies after the last molt takes place. Inside the cocoon, the pupa is covered by a hard shell something like the butterfly's chrysalis. Some moth pupae are not covered by cocoons, but instead are protected by being hidden within crevices in trees or plants or even under a layer of soil.

Within their various hiding places, butterfly and moth pupae remain motionless while the remarkable transformation of their bodies takes place. The process may take anywhere from a few days to half a year, depending on the species. Butterflies that pupate in the autumn have a particularly long period of development because they often spend the winter in the inactive state known as *hibernation*. (Other butterflies and moths hibernate at different stages of their life cycles.) With the coming of spring, the pupae's development is completed and the full-grown *adults* are ready to emerge.

When the adult butterfly or moth first breaks out of its pupal shell, it doesn't look much like the beautiful winged creature we might expect. All its body parts are developed, but they are crumpled and soft, especially the wings, which look like small, limp pads. The adult's body quickly begins to harden, however, as air and blood are pumped through it. The two pairs of wings expand and flatten out, taking on their characteristic colors. Half an hour after it has emerged from its shell, the butterfly or moth is ready to try its new wings.

In their adult forms, butterflies and moths live for no longer than a year, and some survive for only a few weeks. During this time, the insects feed on the nectar of flowers and drink water from pools and puddles. After the adults have mated and laid their eggs, their brief lives are over, and the next generation of butterflies and moths is ready to begin the unique process of development that will take them from egg to larva to pupa to adult.

A beautiful adult butterfly, the Baltimore *(Euphydryas phaeton borealis)*

The Colors of Butterflies and Moths

The wings of butterflies and moths are colorful works of art. Some of the colors on the wings, including the reds, yellows, and oranges, come from *pigments* in the insects' bodies. Pigments are chemicals that create color, and different pigments produce different colors.

The physical makeup of wings also affects their coloring. Each wing is covered with thousands of tiny, overlapping scales. The scales look like shingles on a roof when seen under a microscope. As light hits the scales of some butterflies, it is bent and reflected off in many different directions. This causes the shiny blues and purples that appear on such butterflies as the swallowtail (p. 61). It also produces the dark greens found on other species.

Some butterflies even appear to change colors when they are seen from different angles. Changes in the way light hits their scales causes the color changes. Purple emperors (p. 39) seem to go from purple to brown for this reason.

The beautiful colors and designs of butterfly wings serve many purposes. Brimstone butterflies (p. 21) and many other species look like their surroundings. Their patterns and colors protect them from being seen by enemies.

A striking pattern on such butterflies as the monarch (p. 29) serves as a warning to other animals. Most monarchs are poisonous, and a bird that eats one may become ill. In the future the bird avoids any butterflies with the same coloring as the one that made it sick.

The colors and designs of butterflies also help them recognize members of their own species. Males are attracted to the colors of females belonging to their species. In fact, some males can be tricked into following a model that is painted to look like the right type of female.

The wings of butterflies are beautiful to see. They are also very important in the lives of these insects.

This photograph shows the thousands of tiny scales on the wings of a saturniid moth.

Brimstone Butterfly

The brimstone butterfly is a herald of spring. It is one of the first butterflies to be called out of hibernation by the sun's warming rays at the end of winter.

Male brimstones are bright yellow or yellow-green with a spot in the middle of each wing. Female brimstones also have spots on their wings, but they are a pale greenish-white in color. Female butterflies are sometimes a different color than males of the same species. This helps males locate a mate of the proper sex during mating season.

After they have mated, female brimstones lay their eggs on the leaves of buckthorn trees and shrubs. As caterpillars, brimstones eat buckthorn leaves. The caterpillars' green bodies and white stripes help them blend with the leaves. The buckthorn is so important to brimstones that its scientific name, *Rhamnus,* has also become part of the scientific name of these butterflies.

The brimstone is a woodland creature. It lives on the edges of forests in such mountainous areas as the French Alps.

During the winter, it hibernates on ivy plants. In contrast to the many types of butterflies that hibernate as pupae, the brimstone hibernates in its adult form. Its yellow-green coloring and the shape of its wings make it look just like an ivy leaf. When it hangs motionless from a vine, it can't be easily seen by birds or other enemies.

Brimstones can be found throughout Europe and northern Africa. They also have many close relatives in other parts of the world. They belong to the family Pieridae, which is known for its colorfulness. Members of this family can be found in the tropics of Central and South America, where they grow to be very large and have brilliant orange and yellow colors. Other Pieridae can survive in the cold Arctic. One relative of the brimstone that lives in the United States is the dogface butterfly *(Colias caesonia)*. It is named for the markings on each front wing that look just like the face of a poodle.

Brimstone butterfly *(Gonepteryx rhamni)*

Orange-tip Butterfly

The orange-tip butterfly is named for brilliant splashes of color on the top of its front wings. Only males have this orange coloring. The wings of females are black and white on top.

The undersides of the wings of both sexes have many green spots that are called dapples. These dapples are unusual because the orange-tip doesn't actually have any green scales on its wings. Black and yellow scales, whose colors are created by pigments, blend together to give the appearance of green on the wings.

When the orange-tip is resting, only the dappled green undersides of its wings are visible. This is because the orange-tip, like most butterflies, holds its wings together over its back while resting. This allows only the undersides to show. Since the green dapples blend in well with the surroundings, the butterfly is less likely to be seen by enemies while in this position.

The cardamine plant with its white or purple flowers is a favorite of the orange-tip and gives this butterfly part of its scientific name. Females deposit their eggs on this plant, and the eggs hatch into red caterpillars. The young caterpillars eat the cardamine blossoms. Later they turn to the leaves for food, becoming dark green in color to match the leaves.

An orange-tip caterpillar usually becomes a pupa while on the cardamine plant. The pupa has an unusual triangular shape that makes it look just like a thorn sticking to a branch of the plant. It spends the winter in the pupal stage, and a new butterfly emerges the following spring.

The orange-tip used to be known as the lady of the woods. Like the brimstone, a close relative, it lives in woodland areas. It is common throughout Europe and Asia. Another relative, the giant orange-tip *(Hebomoia glaucippe)*, lives in the tropics from India to the Philippines. The Sara orange-tip *(Anthocharis sara)*, one of many other related species, is found in the western United States. It lives on wild radish and mustard plants.

Orange-tip butterfly *(Anthocharis cardamines)*

White Butterflies

Many species of butterflies that belong to the family Pieridae are known as whites. Their basic color is white, but they may also have black, yellow, blue, or red markings. The butterfly on this page is the small white *(Pieris rapae)*. As a caterpillar, the small white especially likes to eat cabbage. In fact, this species is also called the small cabbage butterfly. On the following page is a picture of a close relative, the large white *(Pieris brassicae)*. It is often called the large cabbage butterfly because of its similar food preference.

As their names suggest, small and large cabbage butterflies differ in size. They also differ in color. The small butterfly is yellowish-white, while the large butterfly is snowy white. Both male and female small whites have one gray spot on each front wing. The female large white has two spots on each front wing, but the male has only one. As a caterpillar, the small white is green with yellow stripes. The large white is yellow and black.

Cabbage butterflies like to travel. They often go on a long journey, called a *migration,* shortly after emerging as butterflies. Many species of butterflies are known to migrate. They do this in order to find a better climate, to return to a particular breeding ground, or to move into a new territory that has a good food supply. Sometimes more than 100,000 butterflies travel together. A group of migrating white butterflies looks just like a snow flurry. Large whites may travel for 12 hours each day, and their journey may last for three days. They have been known to cover 250 miles during a migration. At the end of their journey, they settle down in gardens, fields, meadows, or mountain valleys.

In their new homes, male and female whites soon mate. The females then lay their eggs. When possible, females deposit their eggs on cabbage plants. They are also attracted

Small white butterfly *(Pieris rapae)*

to such leafy green plants as collard and mustards, as well as to the flowering nasturtium.

A large white lays 200 to 300 yellow-orange eggs in clusters on the bottom of a leaf. A small white deposits each egg individually. It may lay a total of 200 eggs. In a short time, the eggs develop into larvae. When the young caterpillars emerge, they hungrily attack their host plant.

The large appetites of cabbage butterfly larvae and their attraction to garden plants and crops make them great pests. They can be especially destructive in farming areas. Various ways to control their population without damaging crops are being tried. One natural control is the presence of wasps. Some wasps lay their eggs on the caterpillars of cabbage butterflies. The wasp larvae grow and feed on the butterfly larvae. Certain viruses also kill cabbage butterfly larvae. These viruses are being introduced in some farming areas to limit the butterfly population.

Both species of cabbage butterflies are common throughout northern Africa, Europe, and east to the Himalaya Mountains in South Asia. In 1860 the small white was accidentally brought to Quebec, Canada. Within a short time, small whites began to appear in the United States, where they are now quite common.

One close relative of cabbage butterflies is the great southern white *(Ascia monuste)*. This species lives along the eastern coast of the United States. Its larvae like to eat garden plants like cabbage, kale, turnips, and broccoli. The caterpillars are various shades of yellow and have dark gray or purplish-green stripes. Male butterflies are white with dark borders. Some females are white, but others can be gray or even black.

The black-veined white *(Aporia crataegi)* is another relative of cabbage butterflies. Its wings are pure white, almost transparent, and are lined with black veins. The larvae of this species live in groups and hibernate together over the winter. They stay together after emerging as caterpillars in the spring, and they may even pupate in groups. This species is found from Europe east to Japan. It can be quite destructive in fruit orchards.

Large white butterfly *(Pieris brassicae)*

Monarch Butterfly

The monarch is one of the most familiar species of butterflies in the world. This native of North America is known for its unusually long migrations. A monarch may travel several thousand miles between its summer and winter homes, covering up to 80 miles (128 kilometers) a day during the trip.

Many monarchs spend the summer months in southern Canada, but when autumn brings cold temperatures, they migrate to California, Florida, and other warm places. The butterflies come to the same spots year after year. One favorite location is California's Monterey Peninsula, where people gather every fall to watch the monarchs fly in from the north.

When spring comes, the monarchs leave their winter homes and return to Canada. During and after this journey, the females lay their eggs, which develop into black, yellow, and white caterpillars like the one shown in the picture.

Monarch caterpillars eat milkweed plants, which have a milk-like juice in their stems. While milkweeds are harmless to the caterpillars, the juice of many milkweed species contains a chemical that is poisonous to other animals. This chemical stays in the monarchs' bodies, even after the caterpillars have pupated and become adult butterflies. A bird will become sick after eating a monarch and will avoid this kind of butterfly in the future. Another North American butterfly, the viceroy *(Limenitis archippus)*, isn't poisonous, but it looks so much like the monarch that birds stay away from it as well.

Since monarch caterpillars depend on the milkweed plant for food, adult monarchs can develop only in areas where it grows. Milkweed isn't found in countries such as Great Britain or China, but monarchs are seen in these and other areas far from their birthplaces in North America. Strong winds carry the butterflies to these distant spots. Some monarchs that migrate between Canada and Florida are blown across the Atlantic Ocean to Europe. Monarchs that migrate near the west coast of North America are sometimes blown across the Pacific to Hawaii and even as far as Hong Kong, on the coast of China. Monarchs have also been seen in Australia, where they have been given the name "wanderer" because of their amazing journeys.

Monarch butterfly and larva *(Danaus plexippus)*

Peacock Butterfly

The peacock butterfly is named for its bright markings. The top side of each wing has a colorful spot, called an eyespot, that is similar to the spots on peacock feathers. While this design is very beautiful, it can sometimes be a problem. It makes peacock butterflies easy to see when they fly, so they are often attacked in midflight by birds. Even when the butterflies avoid being captured, holes may be bitten in their wings by hungry sparrows.

Sometimes the bright coloring of the peacock can actually be helpful. When resting, this butterfly usually holds its wings over its back with only their dark undersides showing. If a bird comes along, the butterfly quickly opens its wings to show its colorful spots. It also makes a rustling sound. The flash of brilliant colors and the noise can surprise the attacker just long enough for the peacock to escape.

In addition to having colorful top sides and dark undersides, the wings of peacocks have scalloped edges. Peacocks are nymphalids (NIM-fa-lids), or members of the family Nymphalidae. Many nymphalids have wings with these same characteristics. These butterflies look just like leaves when they hold their wings so that only the dark sides show. Nymphalids often hibernate as adults, and their leaf-like appearance helps them hide from their enemies during hibernation. Peacocks like to hibernate in dark corners. They can sometimes be found quietly passing the winter in a corner of a porch or inside a house.

Peacock butterflies live from Europe east to Japan. They can be seen in forests, parks, gardens, and even high in the mountains. They are especially easy to find near stinging-nettle plants. These plants are favorites of many nymphalids. Females lay their eggs on nettle bushes. After the eggs hatch, the young caterpillars live on the bushes and eat the leaves. In Europe, people who want to attract more butterflies to their gardens grow beds of nettles among the other plants. In fact, the peacock has become so common in European gardens that it is also called the European garden butterfly.

Peacock butterfly *(Inachis io)*

Mourning Cloak Butterfly

The mourning cloak butterfly, sometimes called the Camberwell beauty in Great Britain, is one of the largest, most attractive members of the family Nymphalidae. Its common name comes from its dark, velvety wings, which look like the kind of cloak that used to be worn by someone who was mourning the death of a loved one.

Mourning cloaks can be found near rivers, brooks, and ponds throughout North America and Europe. They are woodland insects, living where birch, willow, elm, and poplar trees grow. Female mourning cloaks deposit their eggs on the leaves of these trees. After the caterpillars hatch, they eat the sap that runs from the bark.

The mourning cloak caterpillar is velvety black with raised white dots. A row of red spots runs along its back, and long spines cover its body. The caterpillars of this species are very sociable. Many of them cooperate to spin a pouch that serves as their resting place between meals.

When a mourning cloak caterpillar is ready to pupate, it searches for a safe place under a tree trunk, between some stones, or inside a crack in the ground. After finding a good hiding place, the larva changes into a pupa. Unlike many species of butterflies, which pupate in the fall and pass the winter in this stage, the mourning cloak usually pupates in midsummer. By late summer, it emerges as a butterfly.

Mourning cloak butterflies are strong, rapid fliers. Many of them wander a great deal, but sometimes a male will remain near his place of birth and establish his own territory. He defends this territory against strangers. Two competing males can often be seen swooping at each other as one protects his area from an intruder.

The adult mourning cloak spends the winter hibernating. As with other nymphalids, its dark undersides and scalloped wings give it a leaf-like appearance during hibernation. In February or March, it is brought back into action by the warmth of spring.

Mourning cloak butterfly *(Nymphalis antiopa)*

Tortoiseshell Butterflies

Several species of nymphalids are called tortoiseshell butterflies. The tops of their wings have yellow, brown, and orange patterns that resemble the designs on the shells of tortoises.

The small tortoiseshell butterfly *(Aglais urticae),* shown on this page, is common in Europe and Asia. As a caterpillar, it lives on nettles. After it becomes an adult, the small tortoiseshell, like most adult butterflies, feeds on the nectar found in flowers. It especially likes the blue, sweet-smelling flowers of a plant that is sometimes called the butterfly bush. This bush, whose scientific name is *Buddleia davidii,* is often planted in European gardens because it attracts many species of butterflies.

In order to drink nectar from flowers, butterflies use a long, slender structure called the proboscis (pruh-BO-sis). The proboscis is like a long nose, and it can be pushed deep into a flower as a butterfly searches for nectar. Most of these insects fly from flower to flower hunting for the sweet liquid.

In addition to being found in Europe and Asia, tortoiseshell butterflies can be seen in the United States. The American tortoiseshell *(Nymphalis milberti)* is brown with red, yellow, blue, and black markings. As a caterpillar it is black and yellow with many stripes, spots, and spines.

The California tortoiseshell *(Nymphalis californica)* lives west of the Rocky Mountains. Its larvae eat the leaves of white-flowered snowbushes. Sometimes many larvae will eat the leaves on all of the snowbushes within a large area. When they turn into adults, the California tortoiseshells migrate in huge groups, searching for new homes with more food for the next generation. These butterflies can seriously damage the plant life in areas where they occur in such large numbers.

Small tortoiseshell butterfly *(Aglais urticae)*

Red Admiral Butterfly

Red admirals live in many parts of the world, including North America, Europe, northern Africa, and Asia. They are wandering butterflies. They often migrate to the north in the spring or summer before laying their eggs. The butterflies that develop from these eggs fly south in the fall to find a warmer climate for the winter.

Red admirals migrate in groups of different sizes, often traveling with other types of butterflies, bees, and even birds. They are especially strong and stubborn fliers. Even when moving directly into the wind, they hold a straight course. If strong winds interfere with their flight, they try over and over to continue on their original course.

Red admirals are nymphalids, and like many of their relatives, they are attracted to stinging-nettle plants. The butterflies suck nectar from nettle flowers, and the caterpillars use nettle leaves for food and protection.

A caterpillar of this species makes a protective shelter for itself by pulling the edges of a nettle leaf together to form a cone. The caterpillar hides inside the cone while it eats part of the leaf. By the time one third of the leaf is eaten, the caterpillar has grown large enough to shed its skin. After molting, the insect moves to a new leaf, forms another shelter, and begins munching again. Eventually the caterpillar grows too large to hide inside one leaf. Then it makes a bigger shelter by using its silk thread to connect several leaves together.

After it molts for the fourth time, a red admiral caterpillar is ready to become a pupa. It pupates while hanging from a nettle leaf. Two or three weeks are spent in the pupal stage before the butterfly is fully developed and able to emerge. Soon after coming out of the pupa, the adult tests its wings and flies off to a new home.

Red admiral butterfly *(Vanessa atalanta)*

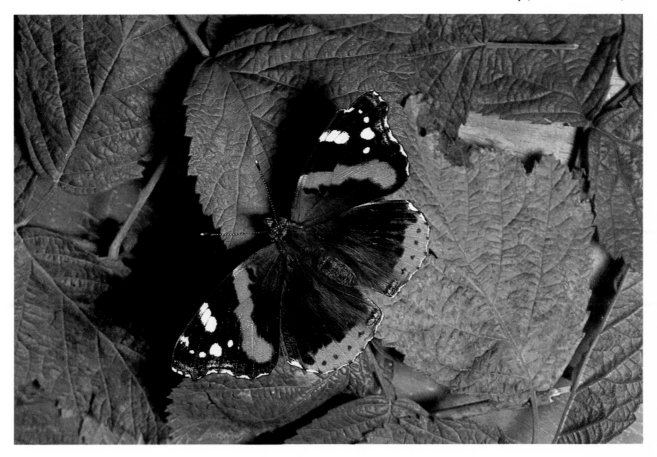

Purple Emperor Butterflies

Glistening shades of purple on the wings of males give purple emperor butterflies their name. Two species of butterflies that look very much alike have this same common name. *Apatura iris,* also called the large purple emperor, is somewhat bigger than *Apatura ilia,* the small purple emperor.

When a purple emperor butterfly moves, it seems to change colors back and forth between purple and brown. The purple appears only when the insect's scales bend and reflect light at certain angles. Brown is seen the rest of the time. In addition, purple colors rarely appear on both wings of the emperor at the same time. Usually if one wing looks purple, the other seems brown. It is hard to catch the light so that both wings bend the rays at just the right angle to create purple.

Both species of purple emperors live from central Europe east through Asia to Japan. There are relatively few members of these species in existence, and they tend to be very shy. As a result, they are rarely seen in large groups.

Purple emperors live in forests and meadows, near ponds or streams. They are powerful fliers. Soaring high in the tops of oak, birch, willow, and poplar trees, they come down only for a drink of nectar from a flower or sap from a tree trunk.

Female emperors spend an especially large amount of time up in the treetops. They lay their yellow eggs on the leaves of trees. Small, dark brown caterpillars hatch from the eggs in midsummer. After their first molt, they look like snails because they turn green and grow two horns on their heads. This appearance protects them from birds, since many birds don't like to eat snails.

When the purple emperor is ready to pupate, it hangs from a leaf and turns into a pale, whitish pupa. Its color and vein-like markings make it look just like the leaf that supports it. Safe from the eyes of enemies, it develops into a beautiful butterfly.

Small purple emperor butterfly *(Apatura ilia)*

Fritillary Butterflies

Many different types of spotted butterflies that live all over the world are called fritillary (FRIT-uhl-air-ee) butterflies. The top sides of a fritillary's wings are often orange and brown with dark spots. Their undersides frequently have brilliant splashes of silver. In fact, 17 species of fritillaries that live in Europe, Africa, and Asia are called silverspot fritillaries because of their markings. The butterfly on this page is a silverspotted fritillary known as the queen of Spain *(Issoria lathonia).* Its spots shine like small reflectors when light hits them at certain angles.

Fritillaries tend to be woodland insects. They are commonly seen in the mountains, flying at high speeds on the edges of forests and in meadows. Sometimes they can also be found in fields and other grassy areas. Many of them are especially attracted to the violets or passionflowers that grow in these areas.

Some species of fritillaries are especially valued by people who collect or photograph butterflies. For instance, the female Diana butterfly *(Speyeria diana)* is noted for its unusual steel blue and black coloring. The Diana is the largest fritillary found in North America, having a wingspan that sometimes reaches 3.8 inches (9.5 centimeters). A Diana caterpillar is shiny black with red, orange, and black spines covering its body. The caterpillar develops from an egg while it is attached to a dead leaf or twig on the ground. Shortly after hatching, it goes into hibernation for the winter. In the spring, the caterpillar searches for a violet plant and lives on the plant until it becomes a butterfly.

The silver-washed fritillary is one of the most abundant silverspotted fritillaries in Europe. It is also one of the largest butterflies

Queen-of-Spain fritillary *(Issoria lathonia)*

of its kind, having a wingspan of 3 inches (7.5 centimeters). Its attractive wings are orange with black spots on the top, and olive green with silver markings on the bottom. Members of this species are found in North Africa and from Europe east to Japan. They generally live in forests of fir and spruce trees.

Adult silver-washed fritillaries mate high in the treetops of their forest homes. Soon after mating, a female deposits her eggs on the bark of a tree. The eggs grow into larvae that remain on the bark while they pass the winter in hibernation. When spring comes, the silver-washed fritillary caterpillars wriggle down from the trees in search of violets. They like to live on these plants, and they spend most of their time eating violet leaves until they are ready to pupate and become butterflies.

Throughout their lives, these and other butterflies are greatly affected by the weather. They tend to be inactive when it is cold and active when it is warm. Even on a sunny day butterflies have to warm up in the morning before they can fly.

In the early morning when the sun is still weak, a butterfly rests quietly with its wings open to the sides. In this position the wings can soak up the greatest amount of sunlight. As the sun's rays become stronger and the butterfly warms up, it raises its wings higher and higher. Only after it has warmed up completely can the insect hold its wings together over its back in the usual resting position. When a silver-washed fritillary has finished warming up, its gleaming silver spots can be seen by anyone who is lucky enough to catch the beautiful display.

Silver-washed fritillary *(Argynnis paphia)*

Map Butterfly

The map butterfly's common name refers to the designs on its wings, which often look like miniature maps. This uniquely marked butterfly is common in southern and central Europe. It also ranges east to Japan.

Female map butterflies have an unusual habit. They deposit their eggs in long columns that hang down from the leaves of nettle bushes. Many eggs are lined up like strings of beads to form the columns. The green eggs soon develop into larvae that vary in color from yellow-brown to black.

Depending upon whether map larvae hatch in the fall or summer, they can become one of two forms of map butterflies. Those that hatch in the fall develop into butterflies like the one shown on this page. With their dark spots on a red-orange background, they resemble silver-washed fritillaries and other species of fritillaries. Larvae that hatch in the summer become black butterflies with broad white bands.

They don't look anything like fritillaries.

The variation in color of the two forms of map butterflies seems to be caused by a difference in the amount of light that shines on the caterpillars. Map caterpillars that hatch in late fall, when the hours of daylight are short, receive only small amounts of light. They spend the winter hibernating as pupae and emerge as the lighter-colored butterflies early the following spring. These butterflies then mate and lay their eggs in late spring or early summer. The eggs develop into larvae that are exposed to a great deal of sunlight during the long summer days. They soon pupate, and within two weeks black butterflies emerge. These dark insects eventually produce eggs that develop into the lighter butterflies the following spring. The scientific name for this kind of difference between members of the same species is *seasonal dimorphism* (die-MORF-ism).

Map butterfly *(Araschnia levana)*

Comma Butterflies

A white mark in the shape of a "c" on the underside of each back wing gives comma butterflies their name. Except for this tiny mark, the wings of commas look just like withered leaves. Their marbled brown coloring and scalloped edges help the insects to avoid being seen by enemies when the butterflies are resting. This is especially important because some commas hibernate as adults and would become helpless victims of hungry birds if they were easy to see.

Many commas of the species *Polygonia c-album* are found from Europe east to Japan. They live on the edges of forests and in gardens. In their larval form, these commas eat the leaves of elm trees, nettle bushes, and hop vines.

A closely related species of comma butterflies, *Polygonia comma,* lives in North America. This species is sometimes called the hop merchant because of its attraction to the hop vine, a plant whose flowers are used in the production of beer.

Like the map butterfly, the comma shows seasonal dimorphism, or variations in color that depend upon the time of year it goes through the larval stage. In the North American species, three different generations of butterflies, called *broods,* may develop during one year. Those that develop in the spring are fairly dark in color. The eggs that they lay develop into even darker butterflies in midsummer. The eggs of the summer brood become adults in September, and these butterflies are much lighter than those of the other broods.

Comma butterflies have many close relatives that differ only slightly in their markings. The question mark butterfly *(Polygonia interrogationis),* found in the United States, has a dot on each hind wing that turns the "c" into a question mark. Larvae of this species are similar in appearance to comma larvae. They have black, brown, and white patterns that make them resemble bird droppings. These larvae are ignored by potential enemies who see them but search for something more attractive to eat.

Comma butterfly *(Polygonia c-album)*

Blue Butterflies

Blue butterflies belong to the family Lycaenidae, and like all members of this family, they are called lycaenids (lie-SAY-nids). Several thousand species of lycaenids are found all over the world.

As caterpillars, some lycaenids eat aphids and other insects, but most prefer the leaves, buds, or flowers of such plants as peas and clover. The color of these caterpillars often matches the color of their food. For example, Chalkhill blue caterpillars *(Lysandra coridon)* are green and yellow. This coloring blends with the green leaves and yellow flowers of the horseshoe vetch, a plant that serves as their source of food and as their home.

Lycaenid caterpillars have several unusual features. They are flatter than most other caterpillars, and their bodies are narrower at both ends than in the middle. Also, many lycaenids have special structures called honey glands on a back segment of their bodies. The honey glands secrete a sweet-tasting liquid that attracts ants. A very close relationship has developed between ants and many species of lycaenids because of this secretion.

Ants like to drink the liquid produced by honey glands. A lycaenid caterpillar often has many ants riding on its back, sucking in the sweet substance. Sometimes a group of ants will even carry a caterpillar to their nest so that they have a dependable supply of food. While in the nest, the caterpillar eats ant larvae and pupae. The lycaenid may live with the ants for a long time, leaving only when it emerges from the pupal stage as an adult butterfly.

As adults, male blues have brightly colored blue wings. The adonis butterfly *(Lysandra bellargus)* shown on this page is a typical example of a male blue. Its color actually protects it from enemies. Birds don't see the color blue very well. They are more attracted to reds, yellows, and oranges, so they are likely to ignore butterflies with blue wings.

In comparison to males, female blues tend to be much less colorful. Their wings are often brown on top. The bottom sides

Adonis blue *(Lysandra bellargus)*

of their wings, like those of males, have dark spots on a background that varies from bright yellow to brown.

Blue butterflies like grassy areas. They can often be found in gardens and in grassy places at the edges of forests. In their home territories, male blues exhibit an interesting behavior called *hilltopping.* During the mating season, they perch on a branch or a rock at the top of a hill, waiting for females to come along. Strange butterflies and other insects are chased away from the area. When a female of the right species appears, the males rush to court her. Many males can be seen following a female, trying to win her attention. Male butterflies of other species are also known to behave in this way during the mating season.

Blue butterflies tend to be fairly small. The dwarf blue *(Brephidium barberae)* is one of the smallest butterflies in the world, with a wingspan of .5 of an inch (1.25 centimeters). It lives in South Africa. The small blue *(Cupido minimus)* shown on this page is the smallest butterfly in Great Britain. It has a wingspan of about .75 of an inch (1.88 centimeters).

Because they are so small, lycaenids usually are not very strong fliers. Some spend their entire lives without moving more than a few yards from their birthplace. The long-tailed blue *(Lampides boeticus)* is an exception to this. While most long-tailed blues live in Africa, continental Europe, and Asia, members of this species sometimes fly across the English Channel to breed in England.

A blue butterfly called the spring azure *(Celastrina argiolus)* is found throughout the United States, Europe, and Asia. As a caterpillar, it lives on dogwood, sumac, lilac, and other flowering trees and shrubs. The larva is very small—a little more than .5 of an inch (1.25 centimeters) long. It has a brown head and a pale body with one dark stripe down its back and several green stripes on each side. The spring azure butterfly is a shining blue in color. It has white bands around the long black antennae on its head, as do most lycaenids. This butterfly visits the blossoms of plum and peach trees to sip their nectar.

Small blue *(Cupido minimus)*

Copper Butterflies

Copper butterflies are closely related to blue butterflies. Like the blues, coppers are very small in size. They rarely have a wingspan larger than 1.5 inches (3.75 centimeters).

Copper butterflies are named for their fiery red-orange coloring. Males and females are similar shades of orange, but they often have different markings. For example, the male large copper *(Lycaena dispar)* pictured on this page doesn't have the many black spots that are generally found on the wings of female large coppers.

"Copper ducat" is another name sometimes used for large copper butterflies. A ducat is a coin, and members of this species do look like copper coins flying through the air. Large coppers live in flower-covered meadows that have a great deal of moisture. They can be seen throughout Europe and parts of the Soviet Union. They used to live in England, in the flat, swampy regions known as fens. When many of the fens were drained for agricultural use, however, the moisture and flowers needed by large coppers disappeared. As a result, these butterflies are no longer found in England. Many other species of butterflies have become extinct in various parts of the world because of similar changes in their surroundings.

The small copper butterfly *(Lycaena phlaeas)* is another species of coppers. Members of this species live in Europe, Central Asia, and eastern Africa. Their front wings look much like those of the large copper. Their hind wings are very dark and have only a few splashes of orange.

The American copper *(Lycaena phlaeas americana)* is a close relative of the small copper. This species is most abundant in the northeastern part of the United States. Its red caterpillars live on sorrel, a leafy plant with tiny red or yellow flowers that is found in pastures, meadows, and along roadsides. Male butterflies of this species are very aggressive. They establish their own territories and will attack larger butterflies or other creatures to drive them away.

Large copper *(Lycaena dispar)*

Apollo Butterflies

Approximately 30 species of butterflies belong to the genus *Parnassius* and are called apollo butterflies. Because they are usually found in mountainous areas, the apollo is also called the king of the mountain.

Apollos belong to the family Papilionidae. Members of this family are known for their exceptional beauty. In fact, the name "apollo" came from the Greek god who represented light, youth, and beauty. Because of their attractiveness, apollos are highly prized by people who photograph butterflies.

The butterfly shown on this page is an apollo *(Parnassius apollo)* that lives high in the mountains of Europe. As a caterpillar, it is velvety black with small blue dots on its back, and orange or red spots on its sides. Members of this species hibernate as caterpillars, becoming fat blue pupae in the spring. During pupation, they lie on the open ground or under stones until they are ready to emerge as butterflies. When they take flight after emerging, they look like pieces of paper floating through the air.

Another species of apollos, *Parnassius autocrator,* lives in the mountains of Asia and is extremely rare. These butterflies are the only apollos to have splashes of yellow on their wings. Most other apollos have white wings that are marked with black and red spots as well as other black designs.

In addition to living in Asia and Europe, apollos inhabit parts of North America and Japan. The large parnassian *(Parnassius phoebus)* can be found in the western United States along with several other species of apollos. Many of these butterflies live in mountain valleys and pastures where stonecrop plants are plentiful. The caterpillars probably feed on these thick-leafed, flowering plants.

Apollo butterfly *(Parnassius apollo)*

Swallowtail Butterflies

Many different species of large, brilliantly colored butterflies are commonly known as swallowtails. Their name refers to the pointed tips, or tails, that most of them have on their hind wings. These tails resemble the long, pointed wings of the birds that are called swallows.

Like apollos, swallowtails belong to the family Papilionidae. The swallowtail on this page *(Papilio machaon)* lives in North America, Europe, and Asia, often in mountainous areas. The caterpillar of this species is green with orange and black spots as well as black stripes. On its neck, it has an unusual orange gland called the osmeterium (oz-meh-TER-ee-um). The osmeterium, which is shaped like a Y, can give off a very unpleasant odor. If the caterpillar feels threatened, it pushes its gland up into the air and releases the strong odor. This keeps away wasps and flies that otherwise might lay their eggs on the caterpillar so that their own larvae could use the insect for food. Many other members of the family Papilonidae have an osmeterium and use it to protect themselves from enemies.

Another species of swallowtail, the tiger swallowtail *(Papilio glaucus),* lives in the southern United States, where it appears in several different color varieties. One is a yellow, black, and blue butterfly similar to the swallowtail pictured here, while another has blue spots on a dark, almost black background. These dark butterflies have very little yellow or orange on their wings.

Tiger swallowtail caterpillars like to eat the leaves of many trees and shrubs, including poplar, ash, and wild cherry trees. Adults are especially attracted to the small, bell-shaped, pink flowers of an ornamental shrub called abelia. This plant is common in gardens throughout the southern United States, and tiger swallowtails are frequent visitors to gardens in which it grows.

Swallowtail butterfly *(Papilio machaon)*

The butterfly shown on this page is the scarce swallowtail *(Iphiclides podalirius)*. It lives in Europe, northern Africa, and Asia. Its name comes from the fact that it is quite rare in Great Britain, Germany, and some of the other countries in which it is found. The scarce swallowtail has a particularly elegant way of flying that has led the Germans to call it the sail butterfly. At times, it sails in the air for up to 30 seconds without moving its wings. It glides along in an effortless flight, carried by the breezes.

In its larval form, the scarce swallowtail lives on hawthorn, apple, pear, and other fruit trees. Female butterflies lay their yellow or green eggs on these trees. Later, green caterpillars with yellow stripes emerge and begin feeding on their host trees. If the caterpillars are ready to pupate in the summer, they remain green during this next stage. Fall pupae are brown and go into hibernation for the winter before emerging as butterflies the next spring.

The scarce swallowtail, like most of its relatives, has only one tail on each of its hind wings, but there is one unusual swallowtail with two tails. Appropriately named the two-tailed swallowtail *(Papilio multicaudatus)*, this butterfly is also noted for its size. It is one of the largest butterflies found in the United States, sometimes having a wingspan of more than 6 inches (15 centimeters). Another unusual North American swallowtail is the zebra swallowtail *(Eurytides marcellus)*, whose black-and-white wings look almost like a zebra's skin, except for the brilliant red spot that appears on each hind wing.

Scarce swallowtail *(Iphiclides podalirius)*

The black swallowtail *(Papilio polyxenes asterius),* shown on this page, is found in the United States, Mexico, and northern South America. Another name for this butterfly is the parsnip swallowtail, because its larvae like like to eat parsnip leaves. They also eat the leaves of carrots, parsley, caraway, and fennel.

Black swallowtails vary quite a bit in color both as larvae and adults. The larvae have black bodies with stripes and dots that may be orange, yellow, white, or green. Some adults have yellow dots on a black background, and others look something like the swallowtail on page 57.

Some of the most beautiful swallowtails live in tropical regions. The Malabar banded peacock *(Papilio buddha),* a very rare species, lives in the forests of southern India. It is a glittering, metallic green in color. The African giant swallowtail *(Papilio antimachus)* lives in the tropics of west and central Africa. Males may have wingspans of 9 inches (22.5 centimeters), and females with wingspans of 6 inches (15 centimeters) have been seen. Members of this species live in the tops of huge trees and rarely come down, so they are difficult to find.

Many especially large and colorful butterflies and moths can be seen in the tropics. Their size and brilliance helps members of the same species find each other so that they can mate and produce eggs. In tropical areas, vegetation is very thick and brightly colored flowers grow almost everywhere. This makes it difficult for insects that belong to the same species to locate each other unless they are big and colorful.

Black swallowtail *(Papilio polyxenes asterius)*

Birthwort Butterfly

Birthwort butterflies, sometimes called southern festoon butterflies, are named for the plant they eat while in the larval stage. The birthwort plant is a vine that grows in the area near the Mediterranean Sea, in central Europe, in Asia Minor, and in other places. It belongs to a group of plants in the genus *Aristolochia.* These plants, which grow in moist, warm areas, have red or brown flowers that give off an unpleasant odor.

Like milkweeds, aristolochia plants contain a poisonous chemical. The chemical doesn't harm caterpillars, but it can poison an animal that eats a butterfly having the chemical in its body. Potential enemies of birthwort butterflies learn to avoid these insects or risk becoming ill. Even a bite of one of these butterflies is enough to teach an enemy to stay away. The poisonous chemical in the insect's body gives it a bad taste. A bird might take one bite of a birthwort, but it would rarely continue eating the butterfly unless it was extremely hungry and couldn't find anything else to eat.

The bright red, orange, and black markings and the zigzag patterns on birthwort butterflies serve as warning signals, telling other animals to stay away. Many species belonging to the family Papilionidae have red and black markings on their wings. Most of them eat aristolochia plants, and their colors signal danger to other creatures.

After birthwort caterpillars have eaten their fill of the poisonous leaves of the birthwort vine, they are ready to become pupae. Birthwort pupae are unusual because they hang from their host plants by their heads. The pupae of most other species hang head downward or attach themselves to plants with silk threads that go around their midsections. Birthwort caterpillars pupate in the autumn, spend the winter in hibernation, and emerge as adult butterflies the following spring.

Birthwort butterfly *(Zerynthia polyxena)*

Marbled White Butterfly

The marbled white butterfly is easy to recognize because of the striking checkerboard pattern on its wings. The light areas on this butterfly can be white or pale yellow. The dark areas can be brown or black. Some individuals, such as the one pictured on this page, have light spots on a dark background. Others have dark spots on a light background.

This species of butterflies is found in parts of Europe, northern Africa, and Asia. It is frequently seen in meadows, along forest paths, on the edges of forests, and in pastures.

Caterpillars belonging to this species are mainly grass-eaters, feeding on orchard grass, the tall blades of cattail grass, and similar plants. Female butterflies deposit their white eggs on these grasses during the summer. The eggs develop into larvae within two or three weeks. As larvae these insects hide from enemies during the day and eat at night. When winter comes, they go into hibernation. After waking up in the spring, they pupate on clusters of grass and become butterflies.

Marbled white butterflies belong to the family Satyridae. Members of this family, called satyrids (suh-TEER-ids), live all over the world. As larvae they usually can be seen on grass, where their green or brown colors blend well with their surroundings. As butterflies, many of them have brown coloring. In fact, a number of satyrids are commonly known as browns.

Satyrids generally have rows of eyespots on their wings. Several species found in the United States, including the pearly eye *(Lethe portlandia)*, the eyed brown *(Lethe eurydice)*, and the gemmed brown *(Euptychia gemma)*, have names that refer to these beautiful spots. The pearly eye has many large, dark spots within a lighter band along the edges of its wings. The eyed brown has a row of small eyespots along each wing. Its spots look like bull's eyes. Each one consists of a tiny light-colored area surrounded by several rings of various shades. The designs on this butterfly are very delicately and beautifully arranged.

Marbled white butterfly *(Melanargia galathea)*

Skipper Butterflies

Butterflies belonging to the families Hesperiidae and Megathymidae are commonly known as skippers. Skippers are somewhat different from most other types of butterflies. In fact, they have many of the characteristics of moths. Their heads are thicker than other butterflies' heads, and their wings are narrower and more pointed. When resting, skippers sometimes hold their hind wings down, as do moths, while their front wings point up over their backs. Most butterflies usually rest with both pairs of wings pointing up. Because of their unusual characteristics, skippers are thought to be very primitive butterflies, perhaps having evolved earlier than the other species.

Skippers tend to be very small, with wingspans of about 1 inch (2.5 centimeters). They flap their tiny wings quickly, making a fluttering noise as they fly from flower to flower in search of nectar. Their common name comes from their tendency to skip or dart around while in flight.

The grizzled skipper *(Pyrgus malvae)* shown on this page is a very common insect throughout central Europe. It is found in meadows and bogs. As a pale green caterpillar, it lives on strawberry plants. Like most other species of skippers, it makes a shelter for itself using a leaf on its host plant. The caterpillar does this by pulling the edges of a leaf together to form a tunnel and then fastening the edges with silk threads. It stays inside this tunnel, munching on the leaf whenever it is hungry. Eventually a similar type of shelter serves as a cocoon for the skipper during pupation.

Many species of skippers live in the United States. They are usually brown or orangey-brown in color. The silver-spotted skipper *(Epargyreus clarus)* has a patch of silver on the underside of its hind wings. Its larvae eat leaves of the sweet-smelling locust and honey locust trees. The giant skipper *(Megathymus yucca)* is also called the yucca skipper. As a caterpillar, it bores into the stems or roots of the tall, white-flowered yucca plant. It lives inside the yucca until it pupates and becomes a butterfly.

Grizzled skipper *(Pyrgus malvae)*

MOTHS

So far you have been reading mainly about butterflies. The insects called moths are very much like butterflies in a number of ways. They are similar in appearance, they go through the same stages in their life cycle, and many of their habits are identical to those of butterflies. There are some important differences, however, between these two types of Lepidoptera. For example, most butterflies hold their wings up over their backs while at rest, but resting moths hold their wings down at their sides. Also, most moths fly about at night and remain in one place during the day, while most butterflies, are active during the day and quiet at night.

In addition to behaving somewhat differently, butterflies and moths have differences in their physical characteristics. For example, butterflies have thin, thread-like antennae with thick, club-shaped tips. Moth antennae don't have clubbed tips, and they are often bushy and feathered. Butterflies have slender, smooth bodies, while moths have thick, furry bodies. In addition, most moths have a special structure that connects their front wings to their hind wings and helps the wings work together during flight. This structure, called a frenulum (FREN-you-lum), is not found in butterflies. Finally, while some moths are quite beautiful, most tend to be much less colorful than butterflies.

The moth on this page belongs to one of the most brilliantly colored species of moths, *Rothschildia jacobaeae.* It is a member of the family Saturniidae, and it lives in South America.

Jacoba silk moth *(Rothschildia jacobaeae)*

Cultivated Silk Moth

The cultivated silk moth of the family Bombycidae is probably the most useful moth in the world. Silk made by larvae of this species is used to produce some of the finest fabric in existence.

Silk moth caterpillars (shown here) are called silkworms. When a silkworm pupates, it produces one continuous silk thread that makes up all but the outer layers of its cocoon. If this thread is unraveled, it may be more than half a mile (about one kilometer) long. Silkworm farmers raise many caterpillars in order to collect their silk threads.

In ancient times, silk moths lived only in China, and the Chinese were the only people to harvest silk. Then in the sixth century A.D., two monks smuggled some silk moth caterpillars into Europe, along with a few of the mulberry trees on which the caterpillars fed. This was the beginning of the European silkworm industry. In addition to the silkworms raised by humans during this period, many others continued to live in a wild state in China. Today there are no wild silkworms; all are raised on silkworm farms.

The production of cultivated silk thread begins with the adult silk moths, which are kept in small containers on silkworm farms. In the fall, the female moths lay their eggs on pieces of cardboard or paper. The eggs are stored in a cool place during the winter so that they will not develop into larvae until spring. If the larvae were allowed to hatch in the winter, there would be no fresh mulberry leaves to feed them, and the finest quality silk comes only from caterpillars that eat these leaves. As the mulberry trees begin to sprout in the spring, the silk moth eggs are gradually warmed up. When the larvae hatch, they are placed on trays and given fresh mulberry leaves daily. After one month the larvae are ready to pupate.

The pupating silkworms are allowed to weave their cocoons for about 10 days. Then the silkworm farmers kill most of the pupae and take out the long silk thread in each cocoon. A few pupae are allowed to develop into adult moths rather than being killed. These moths will produce the eggs that will become the next crop of silkworms.

Silkworms are the caterpillars of the cultivated silk moth *(Bombyx mori)*.

Giant Silkworm Moths

The cultivated silk moth isn't the only insect that is raised for its silk. Some of the moths belonging to the family Saturniidae also produce silk that can be made into fabric. Commonly known as giant silkworm moths, these species produce silk threads that are coarser and shorter than those from silkworms of the family Bombycidae. Material made from the threads is very beautiful, but it is not as valuable as cloth made from the threads of cultivated silk moths.

The Chinese silk moth *(Antheraea pernyi),* shown on this page, is a saturniid (sa-TUR-nee-id), or member of the family Saturniidae. It is raised for its silk in India and China. Larvae of this species are black when young, but they turn green after molting. They grow very quickly and in a short time are ready to build their cocoons. These cocoons are then harvested by silk farmers.

Chinese silk moths have been mated with other, closely related moths in an attempt to improve the quality of their silk. Originally their silk threads were various shades of brown in color. Now the larvae of some of these moths are producing gray, white and yellow threads that are more similar in color to the threads from cultivated silk moth larvae.

Attempts have been made to harvest silk from the cocoons of other saturniid species. The polyphemus (pol-eh-FEE-mus) moth *(Antheraea polyphemous)* of North America has been raised for its silk thread, but so far efforts to make cloth from its silk have failed. In its larval form, this insect feeds

72

Chinese silk moth *(Antheraea pernyi)*

on the leaves of willow, oak, apple, and hawthorn trees. As an adult, it is somewhat similar in appearance to the Chinese silk moth. Its wings vary from reddish-brown to light brown or gray in color. The polyphemus moth has a large eyespot on both hind wings, and a smaller spot on both front wings. Its common name comes from Greek mythology. Polyphemus was the one-eyed giant who was blinded by Odysseus, the hero of Homer's *Odyssey.*

The tree-of-heaven silk moth *(Philosamia cynthia),* also called the cynthia moth, is another giant silkworm moth that has been raised by silk farmers. It was imported from China to the United States in the 1860s. Breeders hoped that silk farming with larvae of this species would become a large industry in North America, but problems developed in producing cloth from the caterpillars'

threads. As a result, it never became profitable to raise these insects. Tree-of-heaven moths are named for the green-flowered ailanthus (ay-LAN-thus) tree, which is sometimes called the tree of heaven. Larvae of this species live on the ailanthus and eat its leaves.

Some species of giant silkworms are not suited for use in silk production because they are difficult to raise in captivity. This is especially true of the many large, colorful saturniids that live in the tropical regions of Africa. (The species shown here, *Nudaurelia zambesina,* comes from the African country of Zimbabwe.) Larvae of these silkworm moths tend to eat only one kind of plant and are not easily kept alive. Some of the African species do not make cocoons at all but pupate in the ground.

The saturniid moths earned the "giant" part of their common name because of their

Giant silkworm moth *(Nudaurelia zambesina)*

size. Most are quite large as caterpillars, as much as 4 inches (10 centimeters) or more in length. In their adult form, the moths are also very big. The cecropia moth *(Hyalophora cecropia)*, sometimes called the robin moth, is one of the biggest moths in the United States. It may attain a wingspan of 5.5 inches (13.75 centimeters). While in the larval stage, members of this species live in forests of maple, birch, oak, elm, and other types of trees. The caterpillars are blue-green with many colorful, raised dots. They hibernate during pupation, attaching their large cocoons to trees. These cocoons are easy to see in the winter, when all the leaves have fallen off of the trees.

The atlas moth *(Attacus atlas)*, pictured on this page, is another very large saturniid. With wingspans that sometimes reach 12 inches (30 centimeters), these moths are among the largest in the world. The only species known to be larger is a close relative of the atlas, the hercules moth *(Coscinocera hercules)*. Hercules moths with wingspans of 14 inches (35 centimeters) have been seen in the rain forests of Australia and New Guinea.

The atlas moth lives in the foothills of the Himalaya Mountains, ranging from India into southern China. Atlas caterpillars eat the leaves of the ailanthus tree, like their saturniid relatives the tree-of-heaven moths. The pale green caterpillars develop into adult moths with unusual patterns on their wings. The tip of each front wing has an eyespot and other designs that make it resemble a snake's head. Perhaps this frightens potential enemies and keeps them away.

Atlas moth *(Attacus atlas)*

Emperor Moths

Many species of moths belonging to the family Saturniidae are called emperor moths. The emperor shown here, *Saturnia pavonia,* ranges from Europe east to Asia. It is the only saturniid in Great Britain. This insect lives in open, shrub-covered areas, where the caterpillars eat heather, a shrub with evergreen leaves and pink or purple flowers. The caterpillars also like other shrubs that have berries and prickly thorns.

To prepare for pupation and hibernation, the emperor caterpillar spins a brown, pear-shaped cocoon that has one open end. Hard bristles that point outward are built into this end, and they keep intruders from entering the cocoon. In the spring, when the newly developed moth is ready to emerge, it secretes a liquid that softens the bristles. Then the insect can slide out of its shelter without being hurt.

As adults, the males of this emperor species are typically orange and brown with large eyespots. The females have the same patterns as the males but are pinkish-gray in color. Unlike most moths, the males fly during the day and rest at night. Females fly mainly at night.

Other saturniids, for example, those belonging to the genus *Automeris,* also have large eyespots. The io moth *(Automeris io),* found in North America and Mexico, has striking eyespots on its hind wings. It is sometimes called the American bull's eye moth because of these markings. When at rest, this moth covers the spots with its front wings so that the bright colors are not visible. If an enemy approaches, the moth opens its wings very suddenly. The flashing eyespots confuse the attacker, sometimes helping the moth to escape. As caterpillars, members of this species use a different method of protection. They have stinging spines that

Emperor moth *(Saturnia pavonia)*

keep other animals at a distance. The spines cause a severe stinging sensation when touched.

The tau moth *(Aglia tau),* shown on this page, is named for white markings found inside each of its four purple eyespots. The markings look like the Greek letter *tau.* This moth is found in the forests of continental Europe, Asia, and Japan. Female tau moths deposit oval, rust-colored eggs on the bottom side of beech, birch, oak, or maple leaves. Pale lime-green caterpillars with red spines hatch from these eggs. After several molts, they lose their spines. When the larvae are ready to pupate, they build a loose cocoon on the ground to protect themselves while they develop into moths.

The behavior of adult tau moths is unusual because it resembles that of butterflies in several ways. Like butterflies, male tau moths fly during the day and rest at night. These moths also rest in the same position as butterflies, holding both pairs of wings up over their backs. They usually sit close to the ground on bushes in this resting position.

Many variations in coloring can occur among tau moths. The picture on this page shows a typical adult, but some insects are much lighter in color, while others are almost black. Also, some have large eyespots while others have tiny spots. It is common among moths to find such variations in the coloring of individuals that belong to the same species.

With a wingspan that rarely is larger than 2.25 inches (5.6 centimeters), the tau moth tends to be rather small for a saturniid. In contrast to it is the giant emperor moth *(Saturnia pyri).* The wingspan of a giant emperor can reach 6 inches (15 centimeters). In fact, this moth is the largest one native to continental Europe. Giant emperor larvae are brightly colored with blue and yellow stripes as well as large, raised blue dots. They feed on the leaves of apple trees and other types of trees.

Tau moth *(Aglia tau)*

Luna Moths

Luna is the Latin word for "moon," and luna moths are named for the moon-like appearance of their eyespots. Along with these beautiful markings, the moths have unusual wing shapes. The back part of each hind wing extends into a long, graceful tail.

The American luna moth *(Actias luna)* lives throughout the eastern half of the United States. As a larva, it eats the leaves of oak, walnut, hickory, and persimmon trees. A luna caterpillar is about 3 inches (7.5 centimeters) long and has a blue-green body covered with multicolored raised dots. When the larva is ready to pupate, it builds a thin, paper-like cocoon against a log or among fallen leaves. It hibernates inside this cocoon and eventually develops into an adult moth.

Several other species of luna moths are similar in appearance to the American species. The Spanish moon moth *(Graellsia isabellae),* pictured here, lives in Spain and France. It has green wings with orange eyespots. It is very rare and in some places is protected by law. Another moon moth, *Argema mittrei,* lives on the island of Madagascar. Males have tails that are up to 8 inches (20 centimeters) long. These beautiful moths are canary yellow and orange in color. Their eyespots are bright orange with black outlines and a black dot in the middle. The cocoons of this species are perhaps the largest of all moths and are made of a shining, silvery silk.

Some luna moths are easy to breed in captivity. This, along with their striking appearance, makes them popular among people who raise moths for scientific and photographic study. In addition to raising the American species, some breeders in the United States are raising the moths from Madagascar. These particular insects must be fed poison ivy as larvae. As moths they require no food. Like many moths, they never eat once they become adults.

Spanish moon moth *(Graellsia isabellae)*

Puss Moth

The puss moth is a notodontid, a member of the family Notodontidae. Notodontid caterpillars are known for their strange shapes and their unusual methods of self-defense.

The picture on this page shows the mature caterpillar of a puss moth. It has a strangely marked head as well as two long, thin tails that extend from its hind end. When this caterpillar is threatened, it brings its tails forward over its back. A red, thread-like strand comes out of the tip of each tail and whips around in the air. At the same time, the caterpillar raises the front part of its body to display its brightly colored head. These actions often scare away enemies. If not, the insect has another way to defend itself. It can spit acid at an attacker and is capable of spraying the liquid for a distance of up to 8 inches (20 centimeters). The acid is secreted by a special gland located just behind the caterpillar's head. With these methods of defense, the puss moth larva has a good chance of growing into an adult rather than being eaten by another animal.

Puss moths live in forests, parks, and other wooded areas throughout western Europe. As caterpillars, they spend most of their time on willow, poplar, and aspen trees. The caterpillars of other notodontids live on trees such as oaks, elms, and hickories. Some of the North American species, such as the saddled prominent moth *(Heterocampa guttivitta)* and the variable oak leaf moth *(Heterocampa manteo),* can do a great deal of damage to forests when their caterpillars feed on the leaves of these trees.

Just after hatching, puss moth caterpillars are dark in appearance. Following the first molt, they have rust-colored backs and green sides. After further development, they take on the colorful appearance of the mature caterpillar shown here. Even in this last larval form, the caterpillars are able to hide from enemies. At rest, they sit on branches in a position that makes them resemble poplar leaves.

The caterpillar of the puss moth *(Cerura vinula)*

When a puss moth larva is ready to pupate, it bites off small pieces of bark from its host tree. It weaves the bark into an extremely hard cocoon using its silk threads. This shelter gives the pupa excellent protection while it develops into a moth. One end of the cocoon is thinner than any other part. When the moth is ready to emerge after pupation, it secretes acid into this thinner area. The acid dissolves the end of the cocoon and the moth slowly works its way free.

Adult puss moths, like the one on this page, pass the day resting quietly on tree trunks or rocks. Their relatively plain coloring helps them avoid being seen by enemies. Like most notodontids, these moths have fluffy bodies, and this fluffiness is probably the source of the species' common name. The moths almost look as if they are covered with cat fur.

An adult puss moth

Lobster Moth

Lobster moths also belong to the family Notodontidae. Their common name refers to the unusual shape of their larvae, one of which is shown on this page. A fully developed caterpillar has exceptionally long legs and a club-shaped hind end that makes it resemble a lobster. Like the puss moth and other notodontids, a lobster moth larva, when threatened, raises the front and back parts of its body in a posture that emphasizes its strange appearance. This helps to scare away enemies and protects the caterpillar from being eaten.

Lobster moths are found in Europe. They live on trees as larvae, so they are most likely to be seen in forests, parks, and along tree-lined avenues. When they first emerge from eggs they resemble red ants in both their appearance and behavior. They gather in clusters on leaves, just as ants do. They also move their false legs in a way that mimics ants. Only after growing and molting do they begin to look like miniature lobsters. In the more developed form, their shape not only helps them to frighten away enemies, but also hides them from the view of other animals. When a mature larva sits without moving, it looks more like a shriveled leaf than like a caterpillar.

The long legs of a lobster caterpillar can create problems for it during molting. Sometimes the insect has trouble pulling its legs out of the old skin. If so, the legs may be bitten off. In this case, new legs soon grow to replace the old ones. Once lobster moths become adults, however, they no longer have this ability.

The caterpillar of the lobster moth *(Stauropis fagi)*

Oak Processionary Moth

The larvae of oak processionary moths, shown on this page, have an unusual habit that is the source of their common name. When these larvae travel from one place to another, they move together in a long line. Each caterpillar carefully follows the one just in front of it so that all of the insects move as if they were in a procession.

Oak processionary moths live in southern Europe and northern Africa and are among the most destructive species of moths found in the region around the Mediterranean Sea. They live on oak trees, and they can cause a great deal of damage by eating the leaves of these trees. One reason processionary larvae are so destructive is that they live together in large groups. They build big nests, and several hundred caterpillars may live in each one. At night, they leave the nests in search of food, with one caterpillar leading while the others fall in line behind it. Sometimes their formation is several yards long. With this many insects eating, the leaves on their host tree can disappear very quickly.

Scientists have done experiments to discover why processionary larvae travel together in their unusual manner. Apparently hairs on the end of the abdomen of one larva touch the insect that is following it and somehow excite the second caterpillar, causing it to continue following the first one. Also, each caterpillar spins a silk thread as it moves, and this thread may be a guideline for the insects behind it to follow.

Another unusual characteristic of oak processionary moth caterpillars is the stinging hair on their abdomens. A cluster of hairs on the middle of the abdomen causes severe itching and swelling when touched. Even if the hairs have been shed long ago and are just lying on the ground, they can still cause a great deal of discomfort to anyone who comes in contact with them. Sometimes molted hairs that are blown about by the wind become troublesome for many people and animals. Farmers have had to bring in their cattle, and people have been forced to leave an area because the hairs were causing so many problems.

Caterpillars of the oak processionary moth *(Thaumetopoea processionea)*

Noctuid Moths

More than 20,000 species of moths belong to the family Noctuidae and are called noctuids (NOK-choo-ids). These moths tend to be dull brown in color. On each side of their bodies, they have an organ called a *tympanic membrane* that allows them to hear sounds. Hearing is important to them because they fly at night and can't see well in the dark.

Many noctuids go on a migration at some point in their lives. The larvae of some noctuids are called armyworms because they march from field to field in huge numbers as they migrate in search of food. Other noctuids, for example, the silver y moth *(Plusia gamma)* shown on this page, migrate as adults. The silver y moth lives in Europe and is named for the silver, y-shaped marking on each front wing. At times, thousands of these moths fly together during the night, migrating to a new territory.

Noctuids are known for their destructiveness. As caterpillars, they often gather in large numbers and destroy entire fields full of crops. The American bollworm moth *(Heliothis zea)* is a particularly destructive species of noctuid that is found throughout the United States. In its larval form, it feeds on cotton, tomato, and corn plants as well as other crops. Farmers often have problems with this insect.

Some noctuid caterpillars are called cutworms due to their habit of cutting off the shoots of young plants close to the ground line. These insects are much more harmful than the larvae of other types of moths because they destroy an entire plant when they eat. Caterpillars belonging to other families usually just eat leaves and are much less likely than noctuids to kill plants as they feed.

Noctuid larvae differ from the larvae of most other species in their living habits as well as in their destructiveness. Rather than living above ground on plants, many noctuid caterpillars live in the soil. They eat the roots and stems of plants. Other species of noctuids stay in the dirt during the day and come out at night to feed above ground on tender shoots. When it is time to pupate, these caterpillars often curl up in the ground without a cocoon. Hidden from the eyes of enemies, they develop into moths.

Silver Y moth *(Plusia gamma)*

Underwing Moths

Many species of noctuids are commonly called underwing moths. This name refers to the brightly colored hind wings that are generally hidden under plainly colored front wings while an underwing moth rests on a tree. If an attacker comes along, the moth suddenly raises its front wings to display the flashy colors of the hind pair. This sometimes startles an enemy and allows the moth to escape.

The blue underwing *(Catocala fraxini)*, shown on this page, ranges from Europe to Japan. It lives in wooded areas. Females of this species lay their eggs inside cracks in the bark of poplar, aspen, and oak trees. The eggs spend the winter in a state of hibernation, and the following spring, caterpillars emerge to eat the leaves of their host trees. The larvae turn into adults that can be seen flying about at night or clinging to tree trunks during the day from June to August.

The darling underwing *(Catocala cara)* is similar in some of its habits to the blue underwing, but it has different coloring. Its hind wings have bright red areas with black bands and yellow borders. Like the blue underwing, it rests on trees during the day. Its brown front wings blend well with the bark of its favorite tree, the maple, so it isn't easily seen by other animals. This insect is found in the northeastern United States. As a caterpillar, it is brown with dark stripes, and it resembles a twig. In daylight, the larva clings without moving to the bark of a tree. Its twig-like appearance helps it hide from enemies.

The white underwing *(Catocala relicta)* is different in coloring from most other underwings. It doesn't have the brightly marked hind wings that are found on other species. Instead, its hind wings are brown with white bands, while its front wings are white with brown bands. It blends well with the bark of its favorite tree, the birch. Members of this species live mainly in the northeastern United States.

Blue underwing *(Catocala fraxini)*

Hawk Moths

Many species of moths that belong to the family Sphingidae are referred to as hawk moths. Most hawk moths are large, swift-flying insects, and they sometimes hover in the air like hawks. They can travel 30 miles per hour (48 kilometers per hour) when in flight.

Most hawk moths need a great deal of food to supply them with enough energy for their flights. Some of these insects have extremely long proboscises to help them locate nectar. The giant sphinx moth *(Cocytius antaeus)* is known for its 10-inch (25-centimeter) proboscis. This moth ranges from South America into Florida and Texas.

Hawk moths of different species show many similar characteristics. For example, at night they tend to cluster by the hundreds around a light. In the morning, large groups of these moths can be found resting quietly near a light. While resting, they remain motionless even if picked up.

As larvae, most hawk moths have a small, brightly colored horn or tail on their hind ends. The presence of this tail makes it easy to identify a hawk moth caterpillar. The larva of the spurge hawk moth *(Hyles euphorbia)*, shown on this page, has a red tail with a black tip. (You can see the tail in the lower right-hand corner of the picture.) Members of this species live in Europe.

The bedstraw hawk moth *(Hyles gallii)*, found in North America, Europe, Asia, and Japan, is a close relative of the spurge hawk moth. These two insects are so closely related that sometimes a male belonging to one of the species will mate with a female of the other species. The bedstraw moth is named for the flowering bedstraw plant, which was used to stuff mattresses long ago. The larvae of bedstraw moths like to eat bedstraw plants.

Unlike the colorful spurge hawk caterpillar, many other hawk moth larvae are green with white stripes. Their plainer coloring helps them blend well with the leaves on the plants that serve as their homes. For example, the five-spotted hawk moth *(Manducca quinquemaculata)* is green and white with a black tail. As a caterpillar, it is sometimes

Caterpillar of the spurge hawk moth *(Hyles euphorbia)*

called the tomato hornworm. Its tail makes it look like a horned worm, and it often lives on tomato plants. It is also found on tobacco, potato, and pepper plants. The five-spotted hawk moth lives in North America. Its adult name refers to five orange spots found on each side of its body.

The eyed hawk moth *(Smerinthus ocellata)* of central Europe, pictured on this page, shows the brightly colored eyespots on its hind wings that give members of this species their common name. These spots are hidden by the brown front wings when the moth is resting. If the insect is disturbed, it pulls its front wings forward to flash its spots. Eyed hawk moths have been seen using this method to startle chickens into letting them escape.

Like tomato hornworms, larvae of eyed hawk moths are colored to blend well with their surroundings. Their bodies are green with markings on the sides that look like the veins of a leaf. These caterpillars also have the typical hawk moth tail.

Many hawk moth larvae can be recognized not only by their distinctive tails but also by their unusual posture. While resting on plants, they often raise the front part of their bodies in the air and withdraw their heads into the connecting segments of their bodies. This is much like a turtle pulling its head into its shell. Some caterpillars sit like this without moving for long periods of time. In this position, they are said to resemble the Egyptian sphinx, a statue with a lion's body and a man's head. Because of this, hawk moths are sometimes called sphinx moths.

The large elephant hawk moth *(Deilephila elpenor),* found in Europe, got its common name because in the larval stage it looks a lot like an elephant's trunk. The elephant hawk moth caterpillar is dark brown, with three pairs of eyespots. When it is frightened, it pulls in its head, and the area with the eyespots puffs out. Then the caterpillar wriggles its body to scare away attackers. Like its relatives, the elephant hawk larva

also pulls its head in while resting.

Another hawk moth, the bee hawk, is unusual because most of the scales on its wings fall off during the adult moth's first flight. As the bee hawk visits bedstraws, honeysuckles, and other flowering plants, its naked, transparent wings and short, thick body make it resemble a bee. The broad-bordered bee hawk moth *(Hemaris fuciformis)* makes its home in Europe, northern Africa, Asia, and Japan.

The death's-head hawk moth *(Acherontia atropos),* shown on this page, doesn't look like a bee, but bees play an important role in its life. This insect eats honey, and sometimes it can go right into a hive full of bees without being attacked. When entering a hive, the death's head hawk moth makes a noise by forcing air through its throat and causing a fold in its mouth cavity to vibrate. The moth's sound resembles the sound made by a queen bee, and it seems to calm down the bees so that they don't attack the invader.

Because of its behavior, the death's-head hawk moth used to be called the bee robber.

Its present common name comes from the yellowish, skull-shaped design on the moth's back. The insect's scientific name also refers to this image of death. The word *Acherontia* comes from "Acheron," one of the rivers of the underworld in Greek and Roman mythology. Atropos was one of the three Fates, the goddesses who controlled the course of human life by spinning thread. When it came time for a person to die, it was Atropos who cut the thread of life.

Death's-head hawk moths live in the tropical regions of Africa and migrate each year as far north as central Europe. Their larvae eat potato, tomato, snowberry, and jasmine plants. The caterpillars are green or yellow with purple stripes and nine blue eyespots. If one of these caterpillars is attacked, it raises the front part of its body, sticks out its front legs, and makes a squeaking sound in an attempt to frighten away the enemy. In central Europe, this caterpillar is sometimes called the wailing mother because of its squeak.

Death's-head hawk moth *(Acherontia atropos)*

Tiger Moths

Tiger moths are brightly colored members of the family Arctiidae. As caterpillars, many different species of tiger moths are called woolybears. This is because of the hair that covers their bodies and gives them a fuzzy, wooly appearance. The hair and the fact that many of the insects are poisonous make them unpleasant to eat. They are generally left alone by birds.

The common or garden tiger moth *(Arctia caja)* on this page is a typical example of an adult tiger moth. It lives in North America, Europe, and Asia. Like most tiger moth larvae, caterpillars of this species shed their hairs when they are ready to pupate. As they spin their cocoons, they weave the hairs in with silk threads to form their shelters. These special cocoons give them excellent protection while they develop into moths.

As adults, tiger moths protect themselves by making special kinds of noises. These moths produce high-frequency sounds, which are so high pitched that humans cannot hear them. The sounds can easily be picked up, however, by the keen ears of bats. Bats prey on moths, but eating a poisonous tiger moth will make a bat sick. After one such experience, a bat will aviod eating moths that make that kind of distinctive sound.

A North American relative of the common tiger moth, the banded woolybear moth *(Pyrrarctia isabella)*, deceives its enemies. It can be safely eaten, but bats think it is poisonous because of the sounds that it makes. Its sounds are almost exactly the same as the noises made by members of tiger moth species that are poisonous, so bats avoid the banded woolybear.

Some tiger moths can be quite destructive when they gather in large groups. One particularly harmful species is the eyed tiger moth *(Ecpantheria deflorata)*, also known as the leopard moth. Larvae of this species feed on the leaves of elm and maple trees. When many of these caterpillars are present in a small area, they can cause a great deal of damage to the trees. As moths these insects have white wings with white eyespots outlined in brown. Their markings resemble leopards' spots. These moths are found in North America from the New England states south to Mexico.

Garden tiger moth *(Arctia caja)*

Burnet Moths

Burnet moths belong to the family Zygaenidae. They are found mainly in moist, warm parts of Europe and Africa. These brightly colored moths fly very slowly in sunny meadows and on grassy hillsides. They are easy to see and to catch, but birds usually avoid them because of their unpleasant taste.

The six-spotted burnet moth *(Zygaena filipendula)* on this page is sometimes called the droplet of blood moth because of its six red spots. Another form of this moth has yellow spots instead of red ones. In Italy, an unrelated species of moths belonging to the family Ctenuchidae mimics the markings of the burnet. Members of this species are known as polka dot moths *(Syntomis phegea)*. A polka dot moth is often avoided by birds even though it doesn't have an unpleasant taste. Birds think it will taste like a burnet moth because it looks like one.

Unlike most moths, burnets fly during the day and rest at night. They live together in colonies and, even when flying about, tend to stay in groups. While hunting for nectar, they gather on flowers in large numbers.

Some relatives of burnets that also live in groups have a very unusual way of eating. These insects are known as western grape leaf skeletonizers *(Harrisina brillians)*. As larvae, they gather in rows on the leaves of wild or cultivated grape vines. They move across the leaves in their rows, gradually eating everything but the veins. When they have eaten their way across an entire leaf, nothing is left but a skeleton of veins. If the larvae are young, both the small and large veins remain. If the larvae are more mature, they eat all but the biggest veins. Moths of this species live in the southwestern United States. As larvae they are yellow with black crossbands, and they have black hairs that sting when touched.

Six-spotted burnet moth *(Zygaena filipendula)*

FAMILIES OF BUTTERFLIES AND MOTHS IN THIS BOOK

BUTTERFLIES

MOTHS

Numbers refer to text pages. Photographs appear on pages shown in italic.

NATURE AND MAN

Other Books in This Series

AMONG THE PLAINS INDIANS, a fictional account based on the actual travels of two explorers who observed American Indian life in the 1830's, features illustrations by artists George Catlin and Karl Bodmer.

AQUARIUM FISH from Around the World presents an exciting picture of the varied species of fish that inhabit the miniature world of an aquarium.

BIRDS OF THE WORLD in Field and Garden combines colorful photographs and an informative text to describe some of the world's most interesting birds.

CREATURES OF POND AND POOL describes many of the beautiful and unusual creatures—frogs, water snakes, salamanders, aquatic insects—that live in and around fresh-water ponds.

DOMESTIC PETS describes the special characteristics of the animals which can live comfortably and happily with man, including several kinds of dogs, cats, birds, monkeys, reptiles, and fish.

WILD ANIMALS OF AFRICA takes the reader on a safari with German naturalist Klaus Paysan, who tells of his adventures in Africa and describes the living habits of the continent's most fascinating animals.

These fact-filled books contain more than fifty four-color plates and over 100 pages. Printed on high quality paper and reinforced bound, these books will add an exciting new dimension to any collection.

For more information about these and other quality books for young people, please write to

LERNER PUBLICATIONS COMPANY

241 First Avenue North, Minneapolis, Minnesota 55401

A Scarlet Macaw, a photograph from *Domestic Pets*